# Contents

KU-015-999

# People in the story

**Jojo:** a ten-year-old boy
**Chris:** takes photographs and writes for an English newspaper
**Doctor Nicky:** the doctor at the Children's House
**Duck:** a UN soldier
**Red:** a boy
**A friend of Jojo's brother**

# Chapter 1 *Only me, Jojo*

It's dark again. So it's evening. It's the third evening. No, I'm wrong. It's the fourth evening.

It's . . . Tuesday . . . Wednesday . . . Thursday. Yes, it's Thursday. Why do I count the days? Why do I say it's Thursday? There aren't any more days. There's just time. Time when it's dark, and time when it's light.

Everything is dead, so why not days, too? Yes. No more days. No more Thursdays. There's only now.

And there's only me. Why? Why aren't I dead, too?

That's a stupid question, Jojo, I say to myself. You know why you aren't dead. You aren't dead because you weren't in the house. You were in the fields when the men came. But that's not my question. I want to know why I was in the fields. Why wasn't I in the house with my family?

There are no answers to questions like that, Jojo, I tell myself. I have to talk to myself because there isn't anyone else. I think there are mice here. I can hear them at night. You can't talk to mice. But there aren't any other people. There's only me. Jojo.

I know this because I listen. I listen all day and all night. I hide in our stable, where the horse lived. And I hear nothing. Just the mice. The village is quiet. There is smoke now, but smoke is quiet. The fires were noisy, but the fires have stopped. It rained yesterday, and after the rain there were no more fires. Just smoke.

Of course, I'm not the only thing alive here. As well as

the mice, there's a dog somewhere in the village. I can hear it. And there are rats and flies. But I think I'm the only person here. All the others are dead.

Everyone in the village is dead. There's only me now and I don't know what to do.

I'm not in our house. I went into our house after the men went away. So I saw my family. All of them on the floor. All the blood on the floor, too. They were all dead. My mother, my father, my sister, my brother. My family.

Jojo, don't think about that, I say to myself. Don't think about the blood. Don't think about those things. But I can't stop thinking about them. My mother had no clothes on. I've never seen my mother without clothes. Perhaps I will go into the house tomorrow and put some clothes on my

mother. She must be cold without clothes. But I'm afraid that the men are going to come back.

Perhaps they are looking for me. Perhaps they will come back for me. Perhaps I want them to find me. Then I can be dead, too. I don't want to be the only one alive.

Come on, Jojo, I say to myself. You are the man of the family now. You must be a big boy. You must be strong.

It's difficult to be strong when you're ten. And I'm only just ten. My birthday was last month. In July.

I got a bicycle for my birthday. It was white. It was a wonderful bicycle. I cycled to school on it every day.

There isn't a school here any more. There was a big fire there and now there's just smoke. I don't know where my bicycle is. But I don't want it any more.

I don't understand why the men came to our village. It's

not a very rich village. We don't have very much. We're not like the people in the big towns. My brother went to live in the town. He told us about the cars and the shops and all the things there.

Why didn't my brother stay in the town? Why did he come back here? Why did he die? He was always laughing. He was always so nice to everyone. He wanted to be a teacher. He went to the town to study. My father said that my brother was a good son. He worked hard. He wasn't going to be a poor farmer like my father. I said I was going to study hard, too, and my father laughed. His big laugh. The laugh that made his tummy go up and down. 'I like that,' he said. 'That's good. I'll have two sons to look after me when I'm old.'

'I'm going to study too,' said my sister.

'Just find a rich husband,' said my father.

'I don't want a rich husband,' my sister told me. 'I'm going to be a teacher like our brother. You see, Jojo, our father doesn't know, but there are lots of women teachers in the town. Our brother told me.'

But my sister can't be a teacher now. She's dead on the floor. There was blood on her legs. I pulled down her skirt. It wasn't nice like that. My sister was always very nice. She was kind, too. Why did the men hurt her? She never hurt anyone.

Sometimes I want to die now, too. But sometimes I don't. I don't want to die.

I sit at the back of the stable. The stable is where our horse slept at night. But the men took away all the horses. I heard them. I'm happy that our horse is alive. She was a good horse. I gave her nuts. She liked eating nuts.

8

I'm very hungry, but I don't want to look for food. I'm afraid one of the men will come back and see me.

I'll stay here and be very quiet. Then no-one will find me.

It's dark now. I can hear the mice. Or perhaps they're rats. I'm not afraid of them. They are probably hungry. I'm so hungry I can't sleep.

Don't think about food. Think about something else. Then I'll forget how hungry I am. Perhaps I'll talk to my mother. Or my brother or my sister. I like to think about them. Perhaps that's why I'm alive. So one day I can tell people about them. I'm Jojo, I'll say. I'm alone now, but once I had a family.

My grandmother said that when people die, they go away very slowly. After they die, they stay in the air so you can say goodbye to them. 'You mustn't be afraid of ghosts,' she told me. 'Ghosts are good. You can talk to them and they will help you.'

I think that there are lots of ghosts here. I think that my grandmother was right.

I'm going to tell them that I'm here. This is Jojo, I'll say. I'm not dead and I won't let the men find me. I'll stay here and I'll talk to you so you won't feel so sad.

Maybe the ghosts will help me.

There's a sound outside the stable. There's something there. Something bigger than a mouse. I don't know what it is. And now I can hear another sound. A bigger sound, like a lorry. It is a lorry. A lorry is coming here to the village. The men are coming here.

I'll be very quiet. Perhaps they won't find me.

# Chapter 2    *The men in the lorry*

The sound outside the stable door changes and I know what it is. *Cluck . . . cluck . . . cluck . . . cluck.* It's my chicken, Whitetail. Whitetail is my favourite chicken. She gives us lots of eggs. 'We're never going to eat her,' my father once told me. He understood that Whitetail was *my* chicken.

I call to Whitetail and she answers me. She comes into the stable, but she's very afraid. Maybe the men tried to kill her. I take her in my arms and talk to her.

'I'm very hungry,' I tell Whitetail, 'but I can't go and look for your eggs because the men are coming. I have to be careful. I don't want anyone to find me.' As I talk to her, I hear another sound, the sound of the lorry. It's getting nearer.

I'm afraid that the men will find Whitetail. Perhaps they will find me, too. And then they will kill both of us. 'You're afraid and I'm afraid, too,' I tell her. She doesn't move in my arms, but I feel a bit better now she's with me. She's happier now, too. She's quiet in my arms.

The sound of the lorry gets very loud. The men are here, outside our farm. I listen and wait.

I can hear lots of voices, but they sound different. They don't sound like the men in our village and they don't sound like the men who live across the river.

I look out through a hole in the wall and I see the men. They aren't the men from across the river. They are soldiers, and they look different. Their clothes and their boots look new, and some of them have red hair. One of them goes into our house. I see him coming out again. He is being sick on the ground. Another older soldier speaks to him. He puts his arm around him. I don't understand what he says, but I think he is nice to the young soldier.

I think that maybe these are not bad men. But I don't know who they are. They have strange voices. I must be careful.

They are looking everywhere. I try to hide in a dark bit of the stable. There is no door because of the fire.

A soldier comes in. He is not old. A little bit older than my brother, I think. He is the young soldier who was sick. Then Whitetail begins to cluck again. The soldier shouts something, but I don't understand. He has a gun. I can't stop Whitetail moving and clucking. I put her down and she runs to the soldier.

He begins to laugh. Whitetail runs out of the stable and the soldier runs after her.

They're going to kill her, I think.

'No!' I shout. I run out of the stable. 'Don't kill her! She's my chicken!'

The soldiers all look at me. I try to move again, but I can't. I haven't eaten anything for days. I fall down.

A soldier picks me up. Now they are going to kill me, I think. But he doesn't look angry. He looks very sad.

He shouts something. Nothing happens. The men are all looking at my house. And then I see another man. He was in my house and now he comes across to me. He doesn't look like the soldiers. He's tall with yellow hair. He has two big cameras. My brother had a camera, but it was very small.

11

The man smiles at me as he walks. He opens his hands to show that he has nothing in them.

'Don't be afraid,' he says. He speaks our language, but he speaks it rather strangely. 'You're safe now,' he says. 'These soldiers won't hurt you.'

'Where's my chicken?' I ask. 'I don't want the soldiers to hurt my chicken.'

The man says something to the soldiers in their language. They laugh and then the young soldier who came into the stable comes to me. Whitetail is in his arms and the soldier gives her to me. The soldier says something and smiles.

The man with the cameras tells me that the soldier comes from a village like mine. His father is a farmer and he has lots of chickens and ducks. But his village is a long way from here.

'What's your name?' the man asks me.

'Jojo,' I tell him. And I tell him that I'm the only one here in the village. He says my words in the other language. He tells me that this is translating. He will tell the soldiers anything that I want to tell them.

I don't want to tell them anything, but the man says that they are here to help.

'Are you hurt?' asks the man with the cameras. He tells me to call him Chris. I tell Chris that I'm not hurt. I was in the fields when the men came.

The soldiers smile at me. They have brown and green clothes, but their hats are blue. It's like a bit of the sky on the top of their heads.

'Are you hungry?' asks Chris.

'Yes,' I say, 'I'm very hungry.'

The soldiers make a small fire for cooking. I can hear it. It's a good sound. The fire in the village was different. It made a sound like the wind at night. A great big wind that makes you hide in your bed with the blanket over your head.

The soldiers give me some rice and beans. It's very good.

'Don't eat it too fast or your tummy will hurt,' says Chris. My mother often said that. I want to cry, but I can't. The tears are all inside my head like a big ball of rice that won't go down.

The soldiers have lots of blankets in the lorry. Chris takes one and puts it over me. I sit down and Whitetail sits down next to me. The young soldier has given Whitetail some food, too. He tells me that his friends call him Duck now, because he has chickens and ducks at home. He smiles at me. I want to smile, but I don't have any smiles any more. The men took them away with them across the river.

I can't feel the ghosts of my family any more. Perhaps they are inside the stable. They don't know that I am outside here with the soldiers.

The soldiers say that I am safe now. I want to believe them. But what's going to happen when they go away and I'm all alone again?

I ask Chris and he tells me that the soldiers are going to take me with them.

'You can't stay here all alone,' says Chris.

I don't know where I'm going, but Chris tells me it's a long way away from the village. He says that I'm going to a place where there are lots of children like me. He says that there has been fighting in other places. And there are lots of children without families. But I have a family. They're here. The soldiers don't understand that. Chris doesn't understand. Only the ghosts understand.

# Chapter 3    *The field of the families*

The soldiers say that they need to bury all the people in the village. This is good. It's not good for dead people to be inside the houses. 'The earth is kind to the dead,' my grandmother always said. 'You must give the dead to the earth.' The soldiers understand this.

'The soldiers need to know the names of the people,' says Chris. 'We need to know who we are burying. Do you know who they are, Jojo?'

'Of course I know,' I say. 'Everyone in the village knows everyone else.'

Chris tells me that he is a photographer and a writer.

'Why are you here?' I ask him.

'Why?' Chris asks. He looks around my village. Or what was my village. 'Because of this,' he says. 'Because men and women and children are dying in your country, and it's important that people outside your country know these things.' He speaks very quietly as if he is talking to himself. 'I take photos because the dead have no-one else to speak for them.'

I understand this. In our village my grandmother always told the stories of the dead. And after she died, the teacher told her story. Now, there is only me here. So Chris is going to tell their stories.

Chris talks to me. He tells me that he comes from a country called England. It's a long way from here. He looks tired. His clothes look tired, too. Maybe he sleeps in his clothes. Chris has a face like tired clothes. Maybe he's travelled a long way.

After I've eaten, I feel stronger. I can stand up. Chris takes me over to talk to the soldiers.

'You must bury everyone in the field of the families,' I tell the soldiers. 'This is where all the families are together. It's very important that the dead sleep with their families.' The soldiers understand. They have families at home, they say.

The soldiers take my family out of the house and I don't want to look, but I do look. The soldiers have put blankets over the bodies. There is no more blood. The soldiers speak very quietly. They don't want to wake up my family. They understand that you have to talk quietly when you are talking to ghosts.

I tell Chris the names of all the people in the village and he writes down their names. Then we go into the field of the families.

We walk round the village. I know all the people in the village. I don't know anything outside the village, and I'm afraid of the world outside. But I don't tell anyone.

I tell the soldiers the names of the people in each house. Then they bring out the bodies.

We go first to the big house. The most important man in the village lived here. He had many cows, as well as goats and chickens. There is nothing here now. All his family are dead. His daughter is dead. She was at school with me. I liked her, she was very funny. She liked drawing. She sometimes drew pictures of the teacher in class.

Now she is a body under a blanket. Next to her is her brother. He was a bit older than me. He went to school, too, and he helped in the fields. He milked the goats in the mornings and evenings, and worked with his father on Saturdays and Sundays.

All my friends. All my cousins and aunts and uncles. All the people I talked to every day. The man with a funny walk, who lived by himself near the river; the woman who gave all the children sweets; our teacher, my family. They aren't here any more. There are only bodies under blankets.

When we go to the teacher's house, we hear sounds. It's the teacher's dog, inside the house. Chris goes into the house and then he comes out.

'The dog isn't hurt,' Chris tells me, 'but he's afraid and very hungry. I can't go near him. Do you know him, Jojo? Does he have a name?'

'I know him,' I say. 'But he doesn't have a name. The teacher just called him Dog.'

'The dog's afraid, but he needs some food and water,' Chris tells me. 'I think that I smell strange to the dog. Perhaps your smell won't be so strange, Jojo. Can you take the dog some food and water?'

I don't know why they don't just kill the dog. He doesn't have a job to do here any more.

'Why don't the soldiers shoot the dog?' I ask Chris.

'They don't want to,' says Chris. 'In my country we love animals. We don't like to hurt them.'

I think I know why they don't want to kill the dog. There are too many bodies here already.

The soldiers have food in little boxes. They open a box and give it to me and I take it inside the teacher's house.

The teacher's body has gone, but there's blood on the floor. The smell of the blood is making the dog very afraid.

18

'Hello, Dog,' I say. 'It's me, Jojo.' Dog is very angry. He wants to hurt me. I put the food on the ground and push it to him. Dog eats it very quickly and drinks the water and I talk to him. After a while, he is quieter. And then I take him outside. He's very happy to be outside and he runs around. He's a nice dog. He's not at all dangerous.

Chris takes photos of me and Dog. He takes photos very quickly. When my brother took photos, he told me not to move. But Chris takes photos when I am moving. His camera makes a funny *click click* sound.

The soldiers all like Dog. They give him chocolate. And they give me chocolate, too.

The soldiers and I go to my school. The fire was very big here. There is no school building here any more. But there are also no bodies. The school was closed when the men came.

The soldiers find two books on the floor. They have a few pages which aren't burnt. They give the books to me. The fire has eaten the village. There is nothing here now. Only me and Dog and Whitetail and two books with black pages.

I show Chris the books and he looks very sad.

'My children read books like that,' he tells me.

The soldiers go into the field of the families. They make holes and bury the people from my village. Then they write their names on bits of wood and push the bits of wood into the earth, too. I go into the field with them. I want to talk to my grandmother.

'Hello, grandmother,' I say. 'This is Jojo. I've brought you the family. I know you'll be happy to see them again. I'm not coming with them. But I want to be with them,

grandmother. I'm all alone here. Well, not really alone. There are lots of soldiers. They don't speak our language, so they can't talk to you. They're nice to me, but they say they're going to take me away. I don't want to leave you, grandmother, but I know I have to go. So I'm here to say goodbye.'

Above the field I can see big birds in the sky. They are bad birds. Birds that don't sing. The birds that sing have all gone.

I am talking quietly to my grandmother when I hear sounds. They are a long way away, but I know what they are. Guns.

Some of the men who came across the river had guns. I could hear the sound of the guns in the field. They were very loud. When they stopped, I could hear them in my head. These guns make a bigger sound. They're a long way away, but I can hear them.

The soldiers are listening, too. They say that we must leave now. The fighting is getting nearer.

# Chapter 4    *The walls will fall down*

I didn't know about the fighting. All I knew was the village and the things my brother told me about the big town. No-one told me about fighting. There are so many things that I don't know. Right now, I don't know where I'm going. I only know that I'm leaving my village.

Chris has a jeep and he says that he will drive me to the Children's House. I know it's a jeep because my uncle had a jeep once. Chris's jeep is very dirty. That's because the earth roads are wet now.

I get into the jeep with Chris and we follow the soldiers out of our village. I am leaving my home. I am leaving everything I know.

I'm thirsty and Chris gives me water from a strange flat bottle. It's got a kind of coat on it. Chris says that it's a soldier's water bottle and it's like that to keep the water cold.

It's good water. There are no flies in it and it's not green like the water from the river.

'Why do people fight?' I ask Chris.

'I don't know,' says Chris. He sounds very tired. 'I don't know why men fight each other. All I do is take photos and tell stories.'

I love stories. My grandmother often told me stories about our family and what happened a long, long time ago. I tell Chris this.

'I don't write stories like that,' says Chris. 'I write stories about things that are happening now. I write for a newspaper in England. I tell people a long way away about people like you,' he says.

'About me?' I ask. 'Are you going to tell my story?'

'Maybe,' says Chris. 'Is that OK?'

I think about it.

'Yes,' I decide. 'That's OK.'

'My newspaper likes stories about children,' Chris says. He sounds angry, but I don't know why.

'Tell me about your family,' says Chris.

So I tell Chris about my family. I can do that. But I can't talk about the men. There are no words for that. The words don't want to come out. I will never tell anyone about those things.

I tell Chris about my parents and about my brother and sister. I want people to know about my family. Chris says he will tell people all about them. He'll tell them about how my father worried about the rain. He'll tell them how my sister wanted to be a teacher like my brother, and he'll tell them about me and my white bicycle.

I tell him how my mother looked after the house. 'After the fire, a lot of the house fell down. I told my mother all about it,' I say to Chris.

'You told your mother?' he asks.

'Yes. I talked to her ghost. You know that, after they die, people go away very slowly. I don't know a lot about ghosts,' I tell Chris. 'Only what my grandmother told me. She said that you can't see them and you can't hear them, but you know that they're there.'

'I think that your grandmother was right,' says Chris.

'When you go to a village after people die you can feel them there.'

I'm happy that Chris understands. I like Chris. He is my new friend. I think he understands. He says that he often comes to my country. He likes it very much. I tell Chris that I'm worried about my house.

'I'm not there now,' I tell him. 'Perhaps all the walls will fall down. Then there will be no more house.'

'I'm sorry,' says Chris. 'But you can't stay there. It's too close to the fighting.'

'When I was a very small boy,' I tell Chris, 'I didn't know why there were walls, so I asked my mother.'

'What did she say?' Chris asks me.

'She told me that the walls hold up the roof, and you need the roof so you don't get wet when it rains. So I went outside to look at the roof, but it was raining and I got very wet.'

Chris laughs.

'I was very small,' I tell him. 'I asked my mother lots of questions and she always knew the answers.'

'My children were the same. They always asked me lots of questions, but I don't think I always knew the answers,' says Chris.

'But we also had walls outside, all the way round the farm,' I tell Chris. 'You saw them. When I was small, I walked round them and thought that these were walls but there wasn't a roof. So I asked my mother why there were walls all round the farm and no roof.'

'And what did your mother say?' Chris asks me.

'She told me that the walls showed that it was our house. We had walls to stop other people from coming in. But I thought, why did we want to stop people from coming in? I didn't understand then, you see. Lots of people came into our house. My father's friends often came in and they drank and laughed together. I heard them when I woke up in the night. And in the morning my father had a headache and we all walked very quietly.'

Chris laughs. I like his laugh.

'I know just how your father felt,' he says. 'When I drink too much, I get headaches, too.'

'My brother had friends in the house, too,' I tell Chris. 'Sometimes people came to buy animals and to sell them. And the doctor from the next village came into our house once when I hurt my head. So I thought and thought. And then I asked my mother about it again.'

'And what did your mother say?' Chris asks again.

'She told me that there were other people in the world. People who weren't nice. She told me that there were people on the other side of the river. They didn't like us and they didn't want us to live on our farms. So we had walls. And my mother told me that the river was our wall, too. It was so big, no-one could cross it. So we were safe. I didn't understand then. I thought, how can a river be like a wall? But I understand now. And my mother was wrong. I thought that she knew all the answers, but she didn't. She didn't know that the people could cross the river. She thought that we were safe. And when the people came from the other side of the river, the walls didn't stop them. The river didn't stop them.'

Chris is quiet. We're going slowly along the road. The road is very bad because of the rain. The guns are louder now.

We're driving past a village and I can see that there has been a fire here, too. It's all black and it smells like our village. It's a very bad smell. We drive slowly, but we see nobody. It's another village of ghosts.

# Chapter 5 *The river*

This is what a dead village smells like, I think. We drive through slowly. There are black birds in the sky here, too. They know that there are bodies here. They want to eat the bodies. Once, one of our cows died in the night. In the morning these birds came and started to eat the cow. They can smell it. The village smells worse than a dead cow. Perhaps all my country smells like this now.

The men who do these things must be very bad.

I can see the river through the trees. We are driving along by the river. I like the river. It's a very big river and it goes very fast. I often walked along it with my brother. He said that you can't swim in it. And if you fall in the river, in two hours you'll be in another country. He told me not to forget that.

I could see how fast it was. I put a piece of wood in the river once and *whoosh* it was gone. I ran along the side of the river, but the piece of wood was faster than me.

It was always quiet near the river. There were trees which looked as if they were talking to the water. The river was a lot of different colours. When it rained, the river was green and grey and silver like the fish that swam in it. On sunny days the river had lots of little gold bits in it. They danced on top of the water as if they were happy that it was a sunny day.

Last month my father and I walked along the river. There was a farmer he wanted to see in another village, and he said that because it was the school holidays, I could go with him. I was very happy. I liked going for walks with my father.

My father often talked to me on these walks. He told me what he was thinking. 'It's too dry,' he said. Or, 'It's too wet.' It was nearly always too dry or too wet. There was always too much rain or not enough rain. When there was too much rain, there were lots of weeds in the fields. My father told me that weeds were green plants that were in the wrong place. They made my father angry. He hated the weeds. And I hated the weeds because it was my job to go into the fields after school and pull them out of the ground.

When there was not enough rain, the fields went yellow and then brown and the ground was hard like the walls of our house. Then all the plants died.

My father and I walked along the river to a place where there were lots of stones.

'There was a farm here once,' said my father.

'What happened?' I asked him.

'The people from across the river came,' my father told me. 'They took all the animals and then made a big fire. And now there's nothing. Just stones and weeds.'

'What about the people?' I asked my father. He didn't tell me.

I know now why he didn't tell me. It was because the people on that other farm were dead. My father didn't want me to know things like that. I can understand that now. Because I know what happens when the men come.

'There's the river,' I say to Chris as we see it again through the trees. It looks different here. It's the same river

as the river near my village, but it's not the same. I think of my mother's face after the men came. It was the same but not the same. I don't want to think about that.

'Do you know any stories?' I ask Chris.

'Oh yes, lots of stories,' he says.

'What's your favourite story?' I ask him.

'It's about some animals who live near a river,' he tells me. 'I'll tell you the story. It begins with a little black mole. The mole lives under the ground.'

'That's good,' I say. 'You're safe under the ground.'

Chris tells me the story. It's about a toad who lives in a big house. One day when he's out, bad animals come into

his house and take it away from him.

'Do the soldiers with blue hats come and help the toad?' I ask Chris.

'No, I don't think so,' says Chris. 'I think that the rat and the mole tell the bad animals to go away.'

'Do they go away?' I ask him.

'Yes,' he says.

'If the soldiers with blue hats ask the bad men to go away, will they go away?' I ask.

'I don't know, Jojo,' says Chris. 'I'll tell you another story,' he says.

He tells me about his house in England. He lives in a

town called Oxford, where there's a big university and everyone rides bicycles.

'Can I come and live with you in Oxford?' I ask him.

'No,' says Chris. 'I'm sorry, Jojo, but I'm not at home very often. I'm always travelling. I never stay anywhere for very long. Today I'm here, but tomorrow I don't know where I'll be. I'll just be somewhere looking for new stories.'

'But you said that your newspaper wanted *my* story,' I say.

'They do,' says Chris. 'They'll love your story. But they want new and different stories every day.'

'I thought you were my friend,' I say. I don't want Chris to go.

'I am,' he says. 'And I'll write to you and I'll come and see you again. And I'll tell you more stories.'

But I don't want to listen to his stories any more.

I can see lights a long way away and I can hear the guns. I'm afraid again.

'Don't be afraid,' says Chris. 'The fighting is a long way from here now. You're safe with us. The soldiers are just behind us.' I look around and see the lorry with the soldiers behind us.

It's night now and I'm very tired. The road is very dark. It goes ahead of us like a river through the trees. Like a dark river.

# Chapter 6  *The Children's House*

It's morning when we get to the Children's House. I'm asleep and Chris wakes me.

I get out of the jeep with Dog and Whitetail, and lots of children run up to see who I am. When they see Whitetail, they laugh.

'Is that your supper?' one of the boys asks me. I have Whitetail very close to me and move back to the jeep.

'Don't worry,' says a woman who comes out of the house. 'No-one's going to eat your chicken. I'm Doctor Nicky,' she says.

There are so many children here. They come from many villages and all of them have stories like mine. That's why they're here. They don't have homes.

'This is your new home,' Chris tells me. 'You'll be fine here.' He says that he knows Doctor Nicky. He met her before in another country. He says that she is very kind and she will look after me.

'Aren't you staying?' I ask him.

'No, Jojo,' he says. 'I'm going to take photos of the fighting. It's my job. But I'll come back as soon as I can. Goodbye, Jojo,' he says. And then he drives away very quickly.

Doctor Nicky shows me round the Children's House. But it isn't just one house. There are many houses where people sleep and eat. And there's a big hospital for all the children who are hurt. There are lots of children here

who are hurt. The house where I sleep is bigger than any house in my village. We all sleep in one big long room.

Days go by and other children come here. We all do lessons together and we play football. Dog likes football, too, but he always tries to eat the ball. It makes the small children laugh. The very small children are happy here because they don't understand what is happening in our country. All the other children are unhappy. I know that because they shout and cry in the night. No-one sleeps quietly here.

Doctor Nicky is the doctor here. She speaks our language very well and is very nice. She wears a white T-shirt with letters on it. 'What are the letters for?' I ask her.

'The letters are for "Médecins Sans Frontières". That means "Doctors without borders",' she answers.

I don't understand. My brother had a T-shirt with letters on it. The letters were the name of our country.

'Is that where you come from?' I ask. I know that some countries are very big. I think that maybe her country is so big that it doesn't have any borders. Maybe it just has sea all around it.

'A land without borders is a good place,' I tell her. 'You can be safe and you won't be afraid of the people who live on the other side of the river. I want to go to the country without borders,' I tell her.

Doctor Nicky smiles. 'No, Jojo,' she tells me. 'It just means that I'm a doctor who will go anywhere. I will help people in any country.'

'Not the country on the other side of the river,' I say. 'You can't help them. They are very bad.'

'But there are children there, too,' says Doctor Nicky. 'They aren't bad. I will go anywhere where there are children who need me.' But I don't want to listen.

I like Doctor Nicky. She has lots of children to look after, but she often talks to me. Many of the children are very ill. Some of the children are here because the men thought that they were dead. But they weren't dead.

There is one boy here who says nothing. No-one knows his name or where he comes from. We call him 'Red' because he has a red T-shirt. Doctor Nicky asks me to talk to Red. I say, 'OK,' but I don't really want to talk to him.

Well, I do want to talk to Red because Doctor Nicky wants me to. But I don't want Red to tell me what he saw.

I'm afraid. I don't want to hear the things that are in his head. I think he's seen some very bad things. I think perhaps he was in his house when the men came.

'There are some things that make you want to stop talking,' I tell Doctor Nicky.

'I know, Jojo,' she says. 'But Red doesn't have to tell us what he saw. I just need to know his name and where he comes from. I need to know if he has a family somewhere.'

'I'll talk to him,' I say.

'So many quiet children and Jojo who never stops talking,' says Doctor Nicky. But she smiles at me and I know she likes me.

I go outside and Dog follows me. Red isn't afraid of Dog, but he's afraid of people.

I sit outside and talk to Red. I talk about my family, tell him stories. I tell him a story about when my mother had a new dress and how it got wet in the rain. She put it near the fire to dry and a bit of wood fell out of the fire and burned it.

Then I tell Red a story about the time my brother went into the fields with the goats, but he started to read a book and the goats ran away.

'I had a goat,' Red says.

'Did your goat have a name?' I ask him.

Red closes his eyes.

'Our goats all had names,' I tell him. But then I stop. I don't want to think about our goats. The men took them away.

'My goat was . . .' Red begins. But he never says what his goat was. He never says any other words. Only those words about the goat.

36

I run to Doctor Nicky.

'Red told me he had a goat,' I tell her.

'Well done, Jojo,' says Doctor Nicky. 'That's a start.'

But it wasn't. It was the end. The next day Red walked out of the Children's House. He walked down the road, between the trees. Maybe he wanted to go home. Maybe he just wanted to go away. I don't know. But I never saw him again.

After he left, Doctor Nicky looked very sad. But then she went back inside the hospital. There are so many sick children.

Some of the children here say that Red stepped on a landmine after he left the Children's House. There are lots of children here who have stepped on landmines. Most of them don't have any legs. Men have put landmines into fields and under the roads. All the places that children go.

I didn't know about landmines, but the other children tell me about them. Landmines sit in the ground and when you stand on them – bang! You die or you get very badly hurt. Often you lose your legs.

Doctor Nicky says that there are thousands and thousands of landmines in our country. When the fighting stops, there will be landmines there. So children will be hurt.

I think about this at night. I also think that the fighting is getting closer. You can hear the guns and also bombs. They're louder than the guns.

At night I think of my home. It's a very long way away. I'm afraid of the bombs and the guns and the sounds they make. I don't want the fighting to come here. I want Chris to be here. I feel safe with him.

# Chapter 7 *Chris*

Chris is here again. He came early this morning. He was wearing the same clothes and looked very dirty. But one of the women here has washed his clothes and now he looks clean again. Chris takes lots of photos of all of us in the Children's House and in the hospital.

The soldiers are here again, too. They don't live at the Children's House, but some of them come and play football with us. Duck likes playing football. He says that he often plays football at home.

Duck tells me that he and the other soldiers come from a place called Ireland. It's near England and it's very green. There are lots of fields, and lots of chickens and ducks. He says that all the soldiers call him Duck now. And it's all because of Whitetail and me. Whitetail likes Duck. Duck picks her up and she clucks very happily.

When the other soldiers are here with Duck, they sometimes laugh at him. They shout Duck's name and then they all laugh.

Chris tells me that 'duck' means two things in English. One is the bird that lives in the water. The other is when you get down on the ground, when someone shoots a gun at you. So the soldiers shout, 'Duck!' and fall on the ground. And then they laugh.

They play games, like me and my brother. I didn't know that soldiers were like this.

'Are the soldiers going to fight the bad men across the river?' I ask Chris.

'No,' says Chris. 'They aren't here to fight. They have come here to try and make the country safe,' says Chris. 'They are United Nations soldiers. They will fight only if someone tries to hurt them. The soldiers come from different countries and they go to other countries to stop people fighting.'

I don't understand. Chris says that the United Nations means that lots of countries get together, like my father did with the other men in the village. They decide all the things that are good and bad and what the other countries have to do. If the other countries don't do them, then they send their soldiers. He says that the United Nations is called the UN. That's what is written on the side of their lorries.

'But the fighting will stop if the soldiers kill the bad men,' I say. 'Then everything will be better.'

'It's not as easy as that, Jojo,' says Chris.

'Why didn't the soldiers come here before?' I ask Chris. 'Why didn't they come here when the bad men first crossed the river? Before my family died? Before the fires?' I think I don't like the soldiers so much now.

'It takes a long time to get the soldiers ready,' says Chris. 'And it's never easy to send men a long way. The important thing now is to stop the fighting. There are villages like yours on the other side of the river, too. And children.'

But I don't believe him.

Chris comes and talks to me every day now. He's teaching me to speak English. He says I'm very intelligent.

'What lessons do you like at school?' Chris asks me.

40

'I like reading,' I answer. 'I'm reading the two books the soldiers found in my old school. They're a bit black from the fire, but you can read some of the pages. When I build a new school for the village, I'll use these books,' I tell Chris.

'When you build your new school, I'll get new books for you,' says Chris. 'I'll ask the people who read our newspaper to give money for the books and for the school.' But Chris looks sad and I know what he is thinking.

He thinks I am a child and I don't understand, but I do understand. He thinks that there is no-one back in the village, so there will never be a school there again.

'There are people from the village who live in the big town,' I tell Chris. 'They'll come back with their children one day and we'll build the village again.'

I remember all the sounds of the village. People laughing and working and talking. The people must go back. I must go back.

When you leave your village, it's like walking into a big hole. You fall and you don't stop falling. And if the village is empty, who will talk to the ghosts?

There are many empty villages in my country. And many ghosts.

The soldiers have made a big hole in the ground and Doctor Nicky makes us hide in it when the sound of the bombs is very loud. All the small children cry.

I want to leave here. I want to go somewhere where there are no bombs and no men with guns.

Chris has been here for two weeks and now he says that he is going away. Not just to another village, but back to England. He comes to say goodbye to me.

'Please take me home with you to Oxford,' I ask him. 'I don't mind if you're not there all the time. I'll study and then I'll make money. I'll make lots of money and come back and build my village again.'

'I'm sorry, Jojo,' says Chris. 'But I can't take you back to England.'

'Why not? I'm very small. I don't eat very much.'

'It's not that. This is your country. This is where you live. I can't . . .' He turns away from me. 'I will try and come back soon,' he says. 'And I will write to you, Jojo.'

And he goes.

I don't want his letters. I want him to take me away. I don't like it here any more.

# Chapter 8   *I knew your brother*

It's two weeks since Chris went away. The fighting is getting nearer. We hear the guns every day now.

And there are planes in the sky. They go round and round like the black birds above my village. When the planes come, we all get into the hole in the ground. Everyone is afraid of the planes. They have bombs. Doctor Nicky says that the roof of our house is white with a big red cross. That shows the men in the planes that this is a hospital.

But three days ago a bomb fell into the trees near the house where all the clothes are washed. Now it's not safe to go inside there and the women have to wash the clothes outside.

Doctor Nicky is angry. Many of the children can't go anywhere because they are too sick.

Every day, when the planes come, we have to hide in the hole. It's very hot there and my head hurts with the sound of the guns and the small children crying.

The sound of the guns goes on all night. It's like the sound of all the trees falling down. It makes my ears hurt. It makes my head hurt. Then, very early this morning, the guns stopped. We went back to our beds and went to sleep.

Today when I wake up, there are lots of men here. They are our soldiers. They look very tired. Some of them don't have any boots and they don't have very much food. They take some of the food that the UN soldiers gave us.

The older boys are very noisy. They talk to the soldiers. Then the soldiers come and talk to all of us. They tell us that we must get bigger quickly, so that we can be soldiers like them and fight for our country.

One of the soldiers comes up to me.

'I think I know you,' he says. 'Aren't you Jojo, the brother of – ?' And he says my brother's name.

'Yes,' I tell him. I know who he is now. He was a friend of my brother's and he came to our village and stayed with us.

I'm very happy to see him. He knows my village and when he talks to me, he talks to me as Jojo who lived in the village. With him, I am Jojo who had a brother.

I understand now why I feel so strange in the Children's House. It's because here I am not really Jojo. When I left my village, I left some of myself there. I was like a snake. I didn't have my old skin, and I didn't have a new skin.

My brother's friend asks about my brother. I tell him. I tell him that I am the only one left from our village. He is very angry. My brother was a good friend of his. He wants to kill the men who killed my brother.

We talk. He tells me what our soldiers are doing. And now, talking to my brother's friend, I feel that I am someone again. I am Jojo and I have a country. A country feels like a new skin.

We talk about his village, too. He says that it is like my village, but it's a long way from here and there isn't any fighting. He says that he will take me there after the fighting is finished. He says that his family are very nice. They will be kind to me. They knew my brother, too.

I like him. He says that he and the other soldiers have

walked for two days without stopping. They are very tired. After we talk, he sleeps on the ground. I look at his boots. They have holes in them. His gun is old, too. It's a small gun. It's not like the big new guns the UN soldiers have. They have new boots, too. And they aren't fighting.

Outside the Children's House, some of the UN soldiers are playing football with the older boys. I see Duck and he smiles at me. Dog is trying to play football, too. I sit and watch them for a while. Dog runs after the ball and catches it in his mouth. Then he runs away. Everyone runs after him.

I am sitting by the wall and Duck's gun and boots are next to me. There is no-one here to see me.

Very quickly, I pick up the big gun and the boots. They're very heavy. I take them to my brother's friend and wake him up.

My brother's friend is very happy when I give him the gun and the boots. He gives me his old gun because he says that I will need it.

He says that our soldiers are going to hide in the hills and I can go with him.

'You can't stay here now, Jojo,' he says. 'They'll be looking for you when they find that the gun has gone.'

I take his old gun. It's not very heavy. I follow him, my brother's friend. He talks to one of the other soldiers who came with him and then he goes through the house and out of the door at the back. There are trees near there and very soon no-one can see us.

I think of Chris as I go. His letters will go to the Children's House, but I won't be there.

I was a boy when I met Chris. That was then. Now I have a gun and I'm a man.

# Glossary of animals

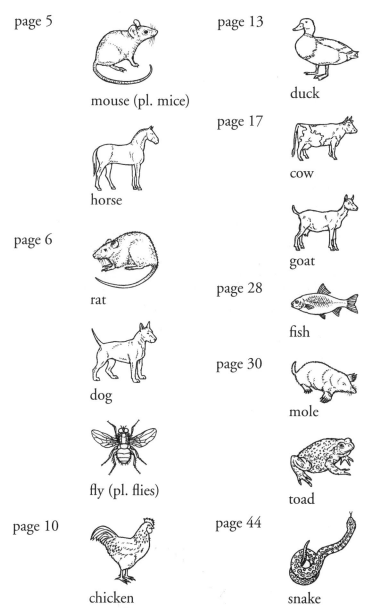

page 5

mouse (pl. mice)

horse

page 6

rat

dog

fly (pl. flies)

page 10

chicken

page 13

duck

page 17

cow

goat

page 28

fish

page 30

mole

toad

page 44

snake

47